A Parent's Guide to Phonics

Understanding How to Help your Child with Reading and Spelling

Ann Sullivan

To: Matthew, Ruth & Tom

With thanks to: Debbie Boekestein, Di Caesar, Val Helliar,
Joanne Holmes, Elizabeth Nonweiler, Lynne Moody,
Kerry Thalia, Julie Upton, Clare Wood and
the late Diane McGuinness

CONTENTS

1 INTRODUCTION

Reading is one of the most important things we can teach our children. Think about all the activities involving reading that we want our children to be able to do:
- read stories, poems and magazines,
- find out information and facts from books and the internet,
- read text in games and online activities,
- read text in the world around them on signs and displays.

As they get older and become young adults, we want them to be able to:
- read the news,
- read about other people's thoughts and opinions,
- read letters and emails,
- understand forms and official documents,
- keep in touch with friends and family on social media.

But there is another aspect to learning to read that is not as immediately obvious as these. As a child moves through school, they learn a wider range of subjects to a greater depth. Learning becomes more specialised, requiring children to find out information about a subject from teachers' presentations on the board, textbooks, the internet and other sources.

Children in upper primary and secondary school are expected to read and write with increasing accuracy and fluency about different subjects. Accuracy means making few mistakes and fluency means reading or writing smoothly, at a good speed and without hesitating or repeating themselves.

So, reading and writing are the tools children need to access the school curriculum. It is important that we set up our children to take advantage of all learning opportunities, so they can make progress and achieve. Being able to confidently read and write impacts on a child's life chances in the long term.

Most people can't remember how or when they learnt to read. At best, we have a vague memory of when we suddenly became able to look at words and read them like we do, almost instantaneously.

Over the past 50 years, there have been lots of approaches to how children are taught to read, some more successful than others. Thanks to research carried out at universities by academics and the work of teachers and practitioners, we can confidently say the best way to teach reading is 'structured phonics'.

Phonics can feel bewildering to parents and other adults supporting a child with their reading. After all, once we can read, it's not something we think about every day, if at all.

The aim of this book is to demystify phonics, making it easy to understand, and to give you tips on how best to support your child on their journey to becoming a fluent reader and speller/writer.

Let's take a closer look at written language and phonics...

→ Foundations of reading and spelling
Notes
→ Phonics is not a method of teaching

2 WHAT IS PHONICS?

Phonics is the name given to the way the foundations of reading and spelling are taught in schools.

It surprises many people to know that phonics is *not a method* of teaching. Phonics is knowledge about how written language is put together and a set of skills that allow us to use that knowledge to read and spell words.

Phonics

Phonics teaches the link between the words we say (or think) and the words we write on the page. It teaches how the letters in written words represent the speech sounds we say in spoken words.

For example, say the word 'cat' out loud to yourself.

When we say that word, we say quite a few sounds, but we say them in rapid succession. We hardly notice the different sounds when we speak so we need to listen carefully and take time to think about them.

Can you hear what sounds you say? You say the sounds /c/ /a/ /t/.

If we want to write the word, we represent each of these sounds by a symbol, which we call a letter.

We 'write down the sounds' using the letters:

c a t

3 sounds   'c' 'a' 't'   c a t

Basically, that's phonics!

There are just a few extra things that we need to know about, though.

Before we look at these, let's think a little more about sounds and letters.

The technical word for the speech sounds in spoken words is **phoneme**.

We write sounds or phonemes in forward slashes so it's clear we are talking about a sound and not a letter. For example, we write /s/ when we talk about the first sound in the word 'sit'.

The technical word for the letters that represent the sounds is **grapheme**.

Some schools teach pupils to use the technical terms 'phoneme' and 'grapheme' others just call them 'sounds' and 'spellings' or 'sound-spellings'.

Find out which terms your child's school uses to talk about sounds and letters and use that with your child. It's good to be consistent.

grapheme / phoneme

Sound = phoneme [4]
Spellings = grapheme

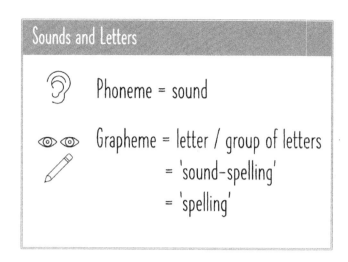

Sounds and Letters

Phoneme = sound

Grapheme = letter / group of letters
= 'sound-spelling'
= 'spelling'

Now let's take a closer look at phonics.

So far, we know that when we write a word, we write a sound-spelling to represent each sound in it. It is like a 'code' that uses the alphabet. In fact, it is often called **the alphabetic code** and it's why reading is sometimes described as **decoding**.   reading = decoding

Very few children can crack the code themselves. They need to be taught it and this is what happens in phonics lessons.

When we speak in English, we use about 44 different sounds in different combinations to make up and say all the many thousands of words in English.

It makes sense then, that in their phonics lessons children gradually learn about the sounds and their matching sound-spellings. They learn to 'crack the code'. Schools follow a programme of study but there are lots of different programmes so find out which one your child's school uses and get to know a little more about it.

5

Working through any phonics programme takes time, up to 3 years, or longer for children with special educational needs, so be patient.

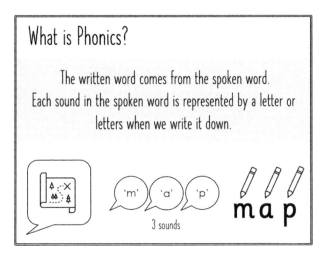

What is Phonics?

The written word comes from the spoken word.
Each sound in the spoken word is represented by a letter or letters when we write it down.

'm' 'a' 'p'

3 sounds

m a p

3 THE ALPHABETIC CODE

When we start teaching a child to read, we begin by keeping things simple. We teach some basic sounds and their matching sound-spellings, as in the word c a t. This gives children the opportunity to learn and understand that written languge is a code, to learn and practise the key skill of blending (more about that later) and to build confidence in their reading.

Wouldn't it be great if we just had to learn one single letter for each of the sounds?

Unfortunately, English is one of the most complicated languages to learn! Here's why....

Some sound-spellings have more than one letter

Have a look these words and notice the letters in bold.

sh o p   **th** i n   s i **ng**

The sounds /sh/ /th/ and /ng/ are represented by sound-spellings that are made up of 2 letters.

It's useful at this point to know that the sound-spellings themselves have been given their own names depending on how many letters are in them. Your child may or may not be taught these names, depending on which phonics programme is used, so check with the school. Sound-

digraph = 2 letters

spellings, such as sh th and ng, have 2 letters and are called **digraph**s.

Now have a look at these words:

trigraphs   *tetragrahs*

l **igh** t   w **eigh** t

The sounds /ie/ and /ai/ are represented by sound-spellings that are made up of 3 and 4 letters.

Sound-spellings which have 3 letters are called **trigraph**s. Sound-spellings which have 4 letters are called **tetragraph**s.

But there is more to think about...

Some sounds are represented by not just one but *lots* of different sound-spellings

Let's look at some words. These all have an /oa/ sound in represented by the sound-spellings in bold.

n **o**   c **oa** t   s n **ow**   t **oe**

th **ough**   c **o** d **e**

As you can see, there are six ways to represent the sound /oa/ in words (the bold letters). Children learn about this in their phonics lessons and find out about the sound-spellings of the alphabetic code for all the sounds.

But there's more...

Some sound-spellings represent *more than one* sound

All these words contain the sound-spelling **ow** but think what sounds it represents in the different words.

b r ow n   s l ow

In brown we say the /ou/ sound but in slow we say the /oa/ sound.

These complications are why it takes so long to learn the alphabetic code and why many children find it difficult, especially at first. It's also why schools use a structured phonics programme that gradually teaches children all about the code, working through the sounds one by one.

Have a look at the Alphabetic Code charts at the end of the book which show you how all the sounds are represented by their sound-spellings.

Don't panic! It all may seem a little overwhelming but remember your child will be working through this gradually at school and will bring reading books and activities home that match what they are doing in lessons - you will work alongside your child and will be able to help and support them.

The Alphabetic Code

Writing is like a code that children need to crack
and know how to use to read and spell.

Children can't crack the code themselves. They need to be taught it.

4 BLENDING

As well as learning how to crack the code, children also need to know how to *use* it to *read* words.

When we read a word, we look at each sound-spelling and match a sound to it. We push the sounds together to make the word. This is called **blending**.

Blending is a skill that children need to be taught and given the opportunity to practice. Being good at blending takes time and lots of practise and experience.

There are two ways that blending is taught in schools.

Firstly, we can teach children to work through the word left to right, looking at each sound-spelling and saying the sound. Then once they have done that, the child goes back, thinks about the sounds again and pushes them together to get the word.

Secondly, we can teach children to work through the word left to right, looking at each sound-spelling and saying the sounds, but pushing them together *as* they move through the word. In this strategy they say the first sound and keep saying it until they're ready to say the next, then say that.

They keep saying that sound until they're ready to say the next, then say it... and so on.

sit  'sit'

In this way the child just listens to the word forming and says what they hear.

You may have noticed that some sounds are easier to blend than others.

Sounds like /f/ /l/ /m/ /n/ /r/ /s/ /v/ /z/ are easy to blend as they can be 'spoken' for a few seconds. When children are first learning to blend this is great because it gives them a tiny bit more time to think about what comes next and do it.

Sounds like /b/ /c/ /d/ /g/ /j/ /p/ /t/ are tricky because we can't 'speak' them for very long without accidentally adding an 'uh' sound. So, when reading, the child must move on quickly from these sounds to the next to avoid that happening. For example, when reading the word bed, the child must move quickly from the /b/ to the /e/ to avoid saying 'bu-e-d'.

It is important that children learn to say the sounds as clearly and precisely as they can to support good blending.

Blending and Reading

To read, children 'decode' the word.

Look at each sound-spelling, one by one, and match a sound for each.
Work through the word, from left to right, push the sounds together and say
what word you hear forming. This is called blending.

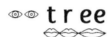 **t r ee**

5 READING LONGER WORDS

When children are first learning to read, we focus on short words to build up their confidence. After a while we can start to introduce longer words.

Longer words are trickier simply because they have more sounds and sound-spellings in. Longer words have so many sounds in that we can't say them in one 'breath'. We say these words in chunks or groups of sounds and when we speak, we can hear 'the beats' within a word.

Let's look at this a little more closely.

Try saying this word out loud: **fun**

You can say all of it in one breath, one beat.   fun

Now try saying: **funny**

Notice you say it in two beats.   fu-nny

Now: **funniest**

Notice you say it in three beats.   fu-nni-est

Chunking sounds together like this is natural to us. Each chunk of sounds within a spoken word is called a **syllable**.

Knowing this and being able to identify the beats or syllables helps us to read longer words.

When we read longer words, we still use blending but in a slightly different way. Now we are on the lookout (or listen out) for a syllable or chunk of sounds.

Let's look at this word: **finish**

The child starts out blending the sounds /f/>/i/>/n/ and at this point can hear that there are enough sounds to make a good chunk or syllable 'fin'.

The child can set this syllable to one side and hold it in their memory. They then carry on with the rest of the word /i/>/sh/ and once again realise they have a comfortable chunk of sounds 'ish'.

Now they have reached the end of the word they can go back and remember the syllables they found and blend those together 'fin'>'ish' – finish.

Having to remember syllables from earlier in the word is the reason why reading longer words is more difficult.

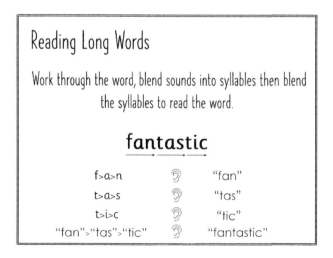

15

6 MOVING ON

With their new and growing knowledge of the alphabetic code and their developing skill of blending, children can 'sound out' words and read them. This is the first step towards becoming a confident, accurate and fluent reader.

But as adults, *we* don't sound out every word, we seem to just look at words and know them straight away. This is called reading *'on sight'*. So, how does this happen? How do children move from slowly sounding out words to being able to read words as soon as they see them?

After lots of research we now understand what happens in the brain when we learn to read words 'on sight'.

Each time a child reads a word by looking at the letters, then thinking about the matching sounds and blending, their brain learns the relationship between the sequence of sounds in the individual word and the sound-spellings that represent them. The sounds and sound-spellings are overlaid and connected in the brain for the individual word.

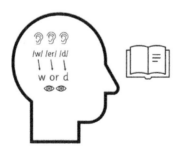

Over time and with repeated practice and experience this information is stored in long term memory. From this point on the information about the word can be quickly recalled when reading and the child can read the word automatically and effortlessly or *'on sight'*.

Lots of experience of reading (and spelling) words is needed for this process to happen so the more practise children get the sooner they will become fluent readers and spellers.

At the same time as the child is developing the ability to read words on sight, they are also learning about how strings of sounds relate to strings of sound-spellings in different words. This information is useful as they can use it later to work out how to read words they have never seen before.

Have a look at this word and read it:

crepuscular

The chances are you've never seen it before as it is an unusual word used by zoologists to describe animals that are active at twilight. Even so, you were probably able to read the word fairly quickly using your knowledge of phonics and of words containing similar strings of letters and sounds.

Alongside being able to read words on sight, as the child learns the alphabetic code and learns how to blend, their reading becomes increasingly fluent. This means that they can read accurately, with good pace (not too slow) and with expression (changes of rhythm and volume that relate to the meaning of the text).

Our children are moving towards becoming fluent readers.

Moving on

As we read, the sounds are overlaid on to the sound-spellings. With repetition this information is stored in our memory in the brain.

Reading becomes automatic. We can read words on sight.

7 COMMON WORDS

We want *all* words to become words that the child can read automatically and without effort, or on sight.

If we think about all the words we read and spell, we can see that some of them are used a lot more often than others; words such as 'the', 'like', 'were' and 'which' pop up in text all the time. These are called the 'high frequency words'.

It would seem to make sense that if children learn these common words early, then it would give their reading a big boost. Unfortunately, many of these words have unusual sound-spellings in them or soundspellings that are generally learnt much later in a phonics programme.

Let's look again at the words above. Notice the bold sound-spellings and think about the sounds.

th e   li k e   w ere   wh i ch

We can see how these are a little more complicated than simple words such as 'cat'.

Some programmes label these common words as 'tricky' or 'common exception' words or even say that they 'cannot be decoded', but this is not true. These words are *inconvenient*, yes, because children meet them early in their experience of learning to read before they have studied many sound-spellings in class. But, if we look carefully at these words, we can easily see the relationship between the sounds and their sound-spellings.

Let's look at an example of a common word that is said to be 'tricky':

said

It has three sounds in it /s/ /e/ /d/. The s and the d aren't a problem for our beginner readers, but the sound /e/ is represented by the sound-spelling **ai** which has two letters and is rare. So how do we deal with this?

Some phonics programmes expect children to learn these words visually as pictures or images of the whole word (without thinking about the sounds and sound-spellings). This is often by done by looking at flashcards of the whole word and then saying the word. Words learnt this way are called 'sight words'.

Earlier we talked about how children learn to read words automatically or '*on* sight' by relating the sounds to the sound-spellings. Now we are using a very similar term 'sight words' to mean learning words as visual whole images. These are two very different things!

We need to be mindful that our teaching follows the science and works with how the brain learns to read. There is a big problem with learning words as 'sight words'. By learning words as whole word images, the sounds and sound-spellings are never overlaid in the brain. So, the child does not learn the relationship between the sounds and sound-spellings in the word. Because of this the brain is not able to extract any information from the word to help read new words with similar letter patterns and strings of sounds.

So, how *do* we deal with these common words early in teaching?

The key is that the teacher or teaching assistant (or parent) identifies the part or parts of the word the child does not *yet* know and give them specific information about just that, encouraging them to then decode the word themselves by blending.

To be able to do this, it's helpful to find out the teaching order of sounds and letters in the school's phonics programme. You will then know what your child has and hasn't studied when you work with them on their reading and spelling.

Here's an example. An early reader encounters this word in their reading book:

is

You know that they have worked on the sound /i/ in class and so you can assume that they know it and can work with it. You also know that they have learnt that the sound-spelling s represents the sound /s/. They have *not yet* learnt that s can also represent the sound /z/ and it this which will cause them difficulties.

So how do you tackle this?

- Encourage the child to start decoding the word and for them to begin by identifying and saying the sound /i/.
- As they move on to the next sound-spelling, gently interrupt them and point to the s sound-spelling (drawing a ring around or underlining it can help the child to notice the sound-spelling).
- Pointing to the s sound-spelling say, 'In this word, this is /z/, say /z/ here.'

- Support the child to start over and blend the /i/ and /z/ sounds together.
- The child can then blend to arrive at the word 'is'.

When supporting reading in this way, there is never a need to simply supply a whole word for your child. You can help them decode every word.

Common Words

Some words are used a lot more than others.

said   the   great
        friend   say

These words can be awkward for beginner readers because they contain unusual sound-spellings or sounds that are studied much later in a phonics programme.

8 READING WITH UNDERSTANDING

Phonics is very much about **de**coding. When a child uses their phonic knowledge and skills to decode text, they 'lift the words from the page'.

But reading is much more than that. Reading is about understanding what you have read: following the story, understanding the facts or information, or getting the message.

We could be forgiven for giving the impression that reading is just about phonics, but teachers and teaching assistants understand that phonics is the foundation, and they include lots of other important aspects of reading into their lessons.

They also work on:
- background knowledge - making sure children know about the subject of the text
- vocabulary - making sure children understand the meaning of the individual words they decode in the text
- language structure - making sure children know and understand the correct order of words in spoken sentences
- comprehension - making sure children learn to read between the lines as well as understand the literal meaning of the text

In school, children work on these aspects of reading with activities often based around talking about what they have read.

At home, encourage your child to ask questions and talk about the book they are reading. As they read, check that they know the background to the story.

For example, if the story is about a fox, they may not have seen one, know that they live in towns and the countryside, know what they eat and so on. This is an opportunity to tell them a little more about and around the subject.

Check that your child knows what all the words mean and give a simple explanation for any unknown ones.

Discuss the story: the characters, the setting, what happens, little details on the illustrations and ask them what they think about the book. If it is a non-fiction book, talk about what they know now and what they knew before reading.

In school, children also learn to 'check themselves' as the read, spotting when they have lost the thread and need to do something to get back on track. Here are some of the things they learn to do to fix things:

1. Ask themselves, 'When did I lose track?' 'Where in the text did it happen?'
2. Ask themselves, 'What is the problem?' 'What happened?'
3. Look back over the text and ask themselves,
   * 'Can I read all the words?' – if not, ask for help with reading a word
   * 'Do I know what all the words mean?' – if not, ask for help with what a word means
   * 'Did I read too fast?' – if so, read it again and take your time

- 'Did I lose concentration?' – if so, read it again - read it out loud if you can
- 'Did I lose the thread of what it means?' – if so, split the text into smaller chunks and work on understanding it chunk by chunk
- 'Did I stop imagining the story in my head?' – if so, read again and imagine a movie of what is happening

Reading and Understanding

Reading with understanding is more than just phonics.

Children need to know:

- the background to the story, poem or text
- the meaning of all the words
- how we order words in sentences to make meaning
- how to read between the lines

9 CHOOSING BOOKS TO READ

There is a wonderful, wide selection of books available for our young readers to look at, read and enjoy. Whether they are interested in stories and poems or factual texts there is something to appeal to everyone.

When children are first learning to read, we need to think carefully about the books we choose to share with them. It is helpful to think about what we want our children to get out of different types of books.

The books that we want children **to read out loud** to practise their reading need to be chosen carefully. We want our children to find success and enjoy the experience of reading a book themselves.

For this purpose, schools use books known as **decodable** readers. They are given this name because they are written to be easy for children to **de**code or read using phonics. The language used in these books is right for the child's age and is chosen carefully to match the child's level of phonic knowledge and decoding skills.

Decodable books follow the phonics your child is learning in class. When reading these books your child should be able to sound out and read most of the words. This is great for building confidence as well as practising reading.

Decodable readers are not the only books that children should experience. Children benefit from us **reading out loud to them**. We could choose any book that might interest them, picture books, stories, poems or factual books. The language used in these books should be right for their age, but it doesn't have to match the child's level of phonic knowledge and decoding skills because there is no expectation that the child reads the text themselves. We do the reading for them. Children often like to look through books afterwards to look at the pictures and illustrations and some children like to recall and retell the story as if they were reading.

Teachers and teaching assistants also choose books that are about the topic or subject the class is studying. Once again, they *read out loud to* the children and encourage them to ask questions and talk about what they have heard.

Decodable readers are great when children are learning to read but there comes a point when they are no longer needed because the child has enough phonic knowledge that they can read any text appropriate for their age. Teachers and teaching assistants know when children are ready to make the move from decodables to conventional texts and will support your child to make the right choice of books.

Choosing Books to Read

Choose books for different purposes.

To practise reading and build confidence:
child reads a decodable reader to you

To listen to books that they cannot yet read themselves:
you read to the child to share the story or poem

To learn about the world:
you read a non-fiction book to the child

10 HELPING YOUR CHILD WITH READING

It takes up to three years for children to learn the alphabetic code and be able to use it to read. Children need lots and lots of practise.

So, what can you do to help and support your child at home?

1. Listen to your child read the books they bring home from school.

2. Encourage your child to point to the sound-spellings as they read. It helps them to notice the relationships between the sounds and the sound-spellings. Pointing to sound-spellings will also help your child to track the words and keep their place.

3. Sounding out each word can be tiring so at the start work in short bursts of 10 minutes or so.

4. Encourage your child to say all the sounds in each word blending them together as they go. Show them how to do it if they need a reminder.

5. Be patient and give your child time to work it out before stepping in to help.

6. If they get stuck on a word, work out where exactly the difficulty is and give them the information they need, usually they have forgotten the sound that matches to the sound-spelling. Then ask them to start again and blend through the word.

7. Support your child when they are reading a common word that contains a rare sound-spelling or a sound-spelling they haven't worked on yet.

8. If you notice your child is sounding out a word that you think they may know 'on sight' give them permission to just say it. Some children are so pleased that they can read by sounding out that they don't realise when they can read words automatically!

9. Read and reread the books your child brings home. Repeated reading of the same book is a great way to develop fluency as well as improving decoding.

10. Talk about and around the story during and after reading. Make sure that your child knows the meaning of all the words in the text, explaining any unknown ones in a very simple way. If they do not understand a sentence in the text, rephrase it so they can find the meaning.

You could talk about:
- the events of the story or the main facts of the text,
- the characters - what they are like, how they might be feeling and why they did some of the things they did,
- the background to the text, for example if the story is about putting on a play at school talk about what a play is, about acting, about the stage and the audience and so on,
- meanings that may be hidden in the text and show how you can read between the lines to work out things that are not obvious straight away.

11. Read lots of stories **to** your child. These may be books you have at home or books from school or the library. These are likely to contain lots of words that your child is not yet able to read because they haven't got far enough into their phonics. Don't expect them to read anything, just let them enjoy sharing the story and pictures with you.

31

11 SPELLING

You now know that writing is a code that uses the alphabet - the alphabetic code. As well as for reading, we also use the code when we spell or write words, we just go in the opposite direction. In fact, spelling is the reverse of reading and can be described as **en**coding.

When we want to spell a word, we think about all the sounds in the word, one by one. We can then match a sound-spelling to each sound, in order, to write the word.

Splitting the spoken word into its sounds before spelling is called **segmenting**.

Segmenting is a skill that children need to be taught and given the opportunity to practise. Being good at segmenting takes lots of practise and experience. The more practise a child has the better they are at knowing which sound-spelling to use for a particular sound in individual words.

Let's look at some examples.

Imagine a child wants to spell the word 'bug'. They identify the three sounds in the word bug /b/ /u/ /g/ and write three sound-spellings:

b u g

Imagine a child wants to spell the word 'fish'. They identify the three sounds in the word fish /f/ /i/ /sh/ and write three sound-spellings:

f i **sh**

Imagine a child wants to spell the word learns. They identify the four sounds in the word learns /l/ /er/ /n/ /z/ and write four sound-spellings:

l **ear** n s

In school your child will be learning how to read and spell using phonics. They use their knowledge of the alphabetic code and their developing skill of segmenting to spell and write words.

As well as spelling words in phonics lessons they will also be doing more and more writing themselves. At first, this will be short sentences and simple phrases on worksheets, but soon they will be writing short stories, poems and recording information about topics and themes.

Segmenting and Spelling

To spell, children 'encode' the word.

3 sounds / phonemes

c a sh

They think about the word they want to write and then work out what the sounds are, one by one. This is called segmenting. For each sound they match and write a sound spelling and so spell the word.

Just as for reading, when spelling longer words it helps to think about the syllables in the word.

The child can listen to themselves saying the word and notice the beats. In this way they can split the word up into chunks of sounds or syllables. They can then work on each syllable in turn, segment it into sounds and match the sound-spellings.

Let's think about this word: 'perfect'.

The first thing to do is to think whether the word can be split into syllables, which this word can be: 'per-fect'.

The child then works on each syllable, one at a time, segmenting and then matching sound-spellings to each sound to spell the word:

Syllable 1:   'per'   Sounds: /p/ /er/
                           Sound-spellings: p   **er**

Syllable 2:   'fect'   Sounds: /f/ /e/ /c/ /t/
                           Sound-spellings: f   *e*   c   t

Now they have written the word:

perfect

Spelling Multisyllable Words

Syllable by syllable segmenting for spelling.

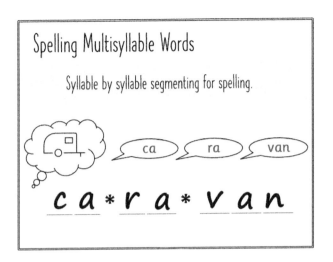

c a * r a * v a n

12 HELPING YOUR CHILD WITH SPELLING

So, what can you do to help and support your child with spelling at home?

1. When your child isn't sure how to spell a word, encourage them to think about the word they want to spell, segment the word, and identify the sounds in it, then write a sound-spelling to match each sound. Finally, they look back and check their work.

2. If your child brings home spellings to practice and learn, encourage them to write out the word saying the sound at the same time as writing the matching sound-spelling.

3. Lines drawn on a whiteboard or piece of paper are helpful – one line for each sound in the word.

$$f\ \underline{a}\ \underline{n} \qquad\qquad \underline{l}\ \underline{i}\ \underline{f}\ \underline{t}$$

4. As your child learns more about the alphabetic code, they will start to spell words that include some of the trickier aspects. For example, imagine your child wants to spell the word 'dream'. The word 'dream' has four sounds in it so you would draw four lines on the paper.

You'd ask them to segment the word and say all the sounds in 'dream' /d/ /r/ /ee/ /m/.

Then ask them to say the sounds again one by one. As they say a sound, they match a sound-spelling and write it on the appropriate line on the whiteboard or paper, like this.

_d_ __ __ __   _d_ _r_ __ __

The sound /ee/ can be represented by lots of different sound-spellings so your child will have to choose the one that is right for this word. Check out the alphabetic code charts at the end of the book. In the word dream the /ee/ sound is represented by the sound-spelling **ea**. Your child may choose the right sound-spelling straightaway or they may need some help.

Imagine your child thinks about the different sound-spellings that represent /ee/ and chooses **ee** and completes the word.

_d_ _r_ _ee_ __

_d_ _r_ _ee_ _m_

Actually, they are **not wrong**! They have remembered and written a sound-spelling that represents the sound /ee/. The point to make, though, is that **ee** is not the sound-spelling that we all 'agree' to use. It is technically correct, but it is not the '**accepted**' spelling. Explain this to them and ask them to think of another sound-spelling for /ee/.

If your child is not sure which sound-spelling to write, you could write down a couple of possibilities and ask them to choose the one they think is the **accepted spelling**. If they are spelling this word before learning about the sound /ee/ in phonics lessons, then simply write **ea** on the line for them at this stage; they will learn about this at a later point.

$$\underline{d}\ \underline{r}\ \underline{ea}\ \underline{m}$$

Familiarizing yourself with the Alphabetic Code charts at the end of this book will help you better support your child in this situation.

Helping your Child with Spelling

Encourage your child to:
- think about the word they want to spell,
- segment the word into sounds
    say all the sounds in the word one by one,
- write a sound-spelling to match each sound,
- look back and check their work.

t ow n

13 CONCERNS ABOUT YOUR CHILD'S PROGRESS

It usually takes around three school years to work through a phonics programme so be prepared to support your child for a good while until they become independent readers and spellers.

Learning to read and spell is one of the trickiest things that children must do and not all children find it easy.

Some children seem to pick up reading and spelling quickly. Others may benefit from some additional teaching. Schools are aware of this, and it is increasingly common to see them providing 'keep up' sessions in addition to the class phonics lessons. When the teacher notices that a child needs a little extra experience of the sounds and sound-spellings being studied or needs extra practise blending or segmenting, then they are directed to short informal extra sessions to enable them to keep up. Children may dip in and out of the sessions as they need to.

Even with the keep up sessions, some children will experience a greater difficulty learning to read and spell. These children may start to lag behind other children in their class and will need additional teaching sessions to be provided on a regular and possibly longer-term basis. Schools call this type of additional teaching an intervention.

These children need to work through the phonics programme at a slower pace so that they can have lots and lots of experience of sounds and sound-spellings. Schools need to make sure they provide phonics teaching beyond the three years usually set aside for initial instruction, so that all pupils complete the programme. With this additional provision and good support to access written work in class, children should still be able to access the curriculum.

If you have any worries or concerns about your child's progress, then speak to your child's teacher sooner rather than later.

14 CHILDREN WITH SPECIAL EDUCATIONAL NEEDS AND DISABILITIES

Some children may have persistent and long-standing difficulties with their learning, including difficulties learning to read and spell. This is because of underlying special educational needs and disabilities (SEND).

Children with SEND are often described as having mild, moderate, severe or complex needs, terms that are helpful for schools and educational professionals as they are a quick way of understanding a child's level of need in general terms.

Teachers and teaching assistants are also aware that every child is unique, and their profile of strengths and needs will be specific to them. They need to find out as much as they can about the individual child so that they can respond well and meet the child's needs in school.

Schools may call in outside professionals to carry out specialist assessments to identify a child's profile of needs and recommend what support and provision needs to be in place. Some children with SEND will be in mainstream school and some in specialist school.

A child may have needs in one or more of these areas:

- learning difficulties, including dyslexia
- autism
- speech
- language

- communication, including pre- and nonverbal children
- sensory
- hearing
- vision
- physical disability
- social and emotional

Learning to read is very important for **all** children, including those with severe and complex needs. Phonics is an important part of this and should be taught to all children. In England the provision of phonics for pupils with moderate to severe and complex needs is written into a document called the Reading Framework which was produced by the Department for Education in 2021. The Reading Framework states that children with SEND should be given appropriate phonics teaching that considers their individual needs and is modified or adapted to enable access to tasks, activities and teaching resources.

Here are some examples of what this might look like:

For children with learning needs, including dyslexia, *lots and lots* of opportunities to learn about the alphabetic code and practice their phonic skills should be provided. A broad range of activities at each level of a phonics programme are required.

For children with autism, teaching should include the use of visual supports (symbols or pictures), be matched to the length of time the child is able to focus and maintain attention on adult led tasks and matched to the child's areas of interest and preferences.

For children with speech and language needs, lessons should include work on spoken and written language structure using the words and vocabulary covered in phonics lessons. Teachers and teaching assistants should work alongside the child's speech and language therapist so that therapy and teaching goals are aligned. Materials should be simple, clear and easy to follow for children.

For children with communication needs, teaching should incorporate strategies that they use to communicate, for example a communication board, talker, E-tran frame or Eye-Gaze system. There should also be strategies in place to allow the child to 'say' what they know and what they need, for example a choice board, visual place marker or signing.

For children with sensory needs, teaching should be set in a suitable environment, be matched to the length of time the child is able to focus and maintain attention on adult led tasks and be delivered regularly but 'informally' rather than to a set timetable.

For children with hearing needs, teacher and teaching assistant need to be aware of the child's hearing profile, particularly which speech sounds the child will be unable to hear even when using hearing aids. When planning phonics sessions this should be taken into consideration and appropriate tasks set. For children who sign, this should be incorporated into phonics lessons.

For children with vision needs, teacher and teaching assistant need to be aware of the child's visual profile and make adjustments as appropriate, for example enlarging text, using magnifiers or providing extra time for tasks. When planning phonics sessions this should be taken into consideration and appropriate tasks set. Some children with no vision will learn Braille instead of alphabetic writing.

For children with a physical disability which affects movement of the upper body, arm and hands, teacher and teaching assistant should provide alternative ways to take part in activities, for example use table-top cards and manipulatives and alternative ways to record work for example using a tablet with an on-screen keyboard or specialist software.

For children with social and emotional needs, teacher and teaching assistant should be aware that they may or may not have some underlying learning needs and respond and plan accordingly. Some children might have gaps in their knowledge and understanding and providing targeted phonics to plug those gaps, enables them to catch up and gain confidence.

Talk to your child's teacher and find out what is in place for your child and what adjustments are made so that your child can access their phonics lessons. You could use these yourself when your child reads to you or does a phonics activity.

It is likely that for children with a higher level or complexity of need it will take much longer to work through a phonics programme. This is because they need more teaching and practice of all the elements of phonics. Don't be worried if your child seems to have been learning phonics for several years.

Life with a child with severe and complex needs is both rewarding and challenging. There are many demands on a parent or carer's time and many struggle from time to time to manage it all.

Don't be too hard on yourself if you can't always find the time to work with your child at home. If possible, try to set aside some time to share books and stories with them, enjoy the shared experience and have fun.

Children with SEND

Learning to read and spell is important for all children. Children with SEND need phonics teaching that considers their individual needs and is modified so that they can access all the activities.

If you have any concerns about your child's progress then speak to their teacher as soon as possible.

---

15 SUMMARY

This book gives you general information about phonics and learning to read and spell.

There are many phonics programmes for schools to choose from, so it is helpful to find out what programme your child's school uses and some information about it. It is particularly useful to find out the teaching order of sounds and how they teach blending. You will be able to keep track of the phonics your child will be working on in class, be prepared for the books your child brings home and be able to help them whenever they need it.

If your child has special educational needs, find out what adjustments the school is making so that your child can access phonics. You can use the same strategies at home when your child does any reading or writing.

If you have any concerns about your child's progress, then speak to your child's class teacher as soon as possible.

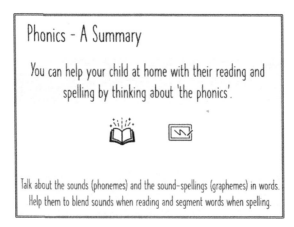

Phonics - A Summary

You can help your child at home with their reading and spelling by thinking about 'the phonics'.

Talk about the sounds (phonemes) and the sound-spellings (graphemes) in words. Help them to blend sounds when reading and segment words when spelling.

APPENDIX

These Alphabetic Code Charts can be used for reference to help you easily see how the code works.

They include:

- A 'Starting Out' chart showing the sounds and sound-spellings your child will learn when they begin to learn to read and spell. This is sometimes referred to as basic code or initial code.
- A set of three 'Moving On' charts showing the sounds and sound-spellings your child will learn as they begin to tackle the more complicated aspects of how the code works. This is sometimes referred to as advanced code or extended code.

There are some things to bear in mind when using these charts.

They are based on generalized English pronunciation and do not account for all regional variations. Be prepared to be flexible. If a word does not fit in with the way you and your child speak then it's fine to move it to another box.

The charts do not show absolutely every sound-spelling for the sounds as there is only space for the main ones that occur commonly. You may come across a sound-spelling that is not shown on the chart, e.g. the **aigh** sound-spelling that represents the sound /ai/ in the word 'straight'.

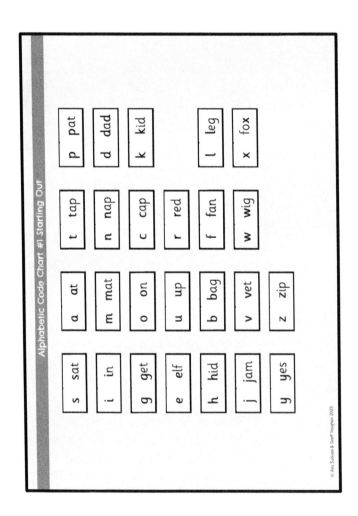

oa	boat		
o_e	home		
o	go		
ow	grow		
oe	toe		
ough	though		

er	her
ur	burn
ir	bird
ear	learn
or	word
ar	collar

oo	book
oul	could
u	push

ie	pie
i	mind
y	by
igh	night
i_e	kite

ou	loud
ow	down
ou	plough

ee	seem
ea	dream
y	happy
e	be
ie	field
e_e	eve
i	ski

oo	moon
u	truth
u_e	rule
ew	grew
o	do
ui	suit
ou	soup
ue	blue
ough	through

or	for
aw	saw
al	walk
a	fall
ore	more
ar	warm
our	your
oar	roar
au	haunt
ough	bought
oar	roar
augh	taught

air	hair
ere	there
are	care
ear	bear

u	up
o	month
ou	touch
o_e	come

ai	train
a_e	made
a	alien
ay	play
ea	great

e	red
ea	head
a	many

i	ink
y	myth

ar	star
a	father
al	calm
ear	heart

u	music
u_e	cube
ew	few
ue	cue

o	lock
a	want

oi	soil
oy	boy

ear	near
eer	deer
ere	here

49

s	sat	m	man	r	rat	th	thin
c	city	mm	summer	wr	wrong		
ss	less	mn	hymn	rr	hurry	ng	ring
st	listen	mb	lamb	rh	rhino		
ce	dance						
se	house	d	dog	h	hat	l	lamp
sc	scent	dd	ladder	wh	who	ll	bell
		ed	wagged			le	little
t	top			b	bat	el	travel
tt	letting	g	get	bb	robber	il	pupil
bt	doubt	gg	wiggle	bu	build	al	metal
		gu	guard			ol	symbol
p	pet	gue	plague	f	fan		
pp	happy	gh	ghost	ph	phone	j	jam
				ff	stuff	g	giant
n	not	c	can	gh	cough	ge	large
kn	knot	k	kid			dge	bridge
nn	sunny	ck	duck	v	van		
gn	gnat	ch	chemist	ve	have	w	wig
		que	plaque			wh	which

x	fox		
xc	except		
cc	accept		
z	zip	sh	ship
s	his	s	sugar
zz	buzz	ch	machine
ze	freeze	ci	special
se	noise	ti	potential
		ch	chips
		tch	match
		qu	quick

50

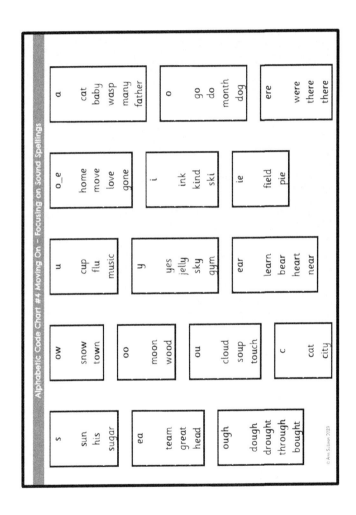

Alphabetic Code Chart #4 Moving On – Focusing on Sound Spellings

a	o_e	u	ow	s
cat	home	cup	snow	sun
baby	move	flu	town	his
wasp	love	music		sugar
many	gone			
father				

o	i	y	oo	ea
go	ink	yes	moon	team
do	kind	jelly	wood	great
month	ski	sky		head
dog		gym		

ere	ie	ear	ou	ough
were	field	learn	cloud	dough
there	pie	bear	soup	drought
there		heart	touch	through
		near		bought

			c	
			cat	
			city	

Printed in Great Britain
by Amazon

29720032R00036